Skya Abbate

Epiphany

an island story

Epiphany
An Island Story
Skya Abbate

Original watercolor paintings by Skya Abbate

Cover and book design: Amor Deus Publishing Design Department

For information regarding permission, write to:
Amor Deus Publishing
Attention: Permissions Dept.
4727 North 12th Street
Phoenix, AZ 85014

ISBN 978-1-61956-257-8

First Edition September 2014
10 9 8 7 6 5 4 3 2 1

Published and printed in the United States of America by Amor Deus Publishing, an imprint of Vesuvius Press Incorporated.
For additional inspirational books visit us at AmorDeus.com

Dedication

To Jennifer,
you are my light.

She lived in a land

surrounded

by sea

where whales' tails waved
"Good Morning"
in thanks to be free

and wild bees made

sweet honey

from bright flowering trees

Here **parrots**

ate **carrots**

and fish

loved

dried peas!

Sea turtles
formed hurdles
from reefs and the seas

Seals and dolphin families
made magic
to please

Coffee grew in the **fields**

sugar in **canes**

rice in the **paddies**

pineapples of **fame**

bananas, papaya

food from the **earth** came

Palm trees
danced aloha
to birds
bowed in trees
The turquoise blue ocean

fell down on its knees
as waves kissed the gold sand
and misted the breeze

She loved to play at Turtle Bay

with dolphins

in the water

She **loved** her cat
horses and bats
to her all were
God's daughters

Child of God, woman and man
she loved the sea, the sky, the land
She sang of freedom, love and cried
through songs she sang
"This is our home, Creation's gift
Life is not dry but earth's and man's"

One day she saw a man
who lived on the street
his clothes were old and torn
he wasn't clean, he wasn't neat
he had no money
nothing to eat

hungry

With sad sick eyes
he asked for care
money or food
from anywhere
She placed lunch money at his bare feet
he smiled a smile
from here to there

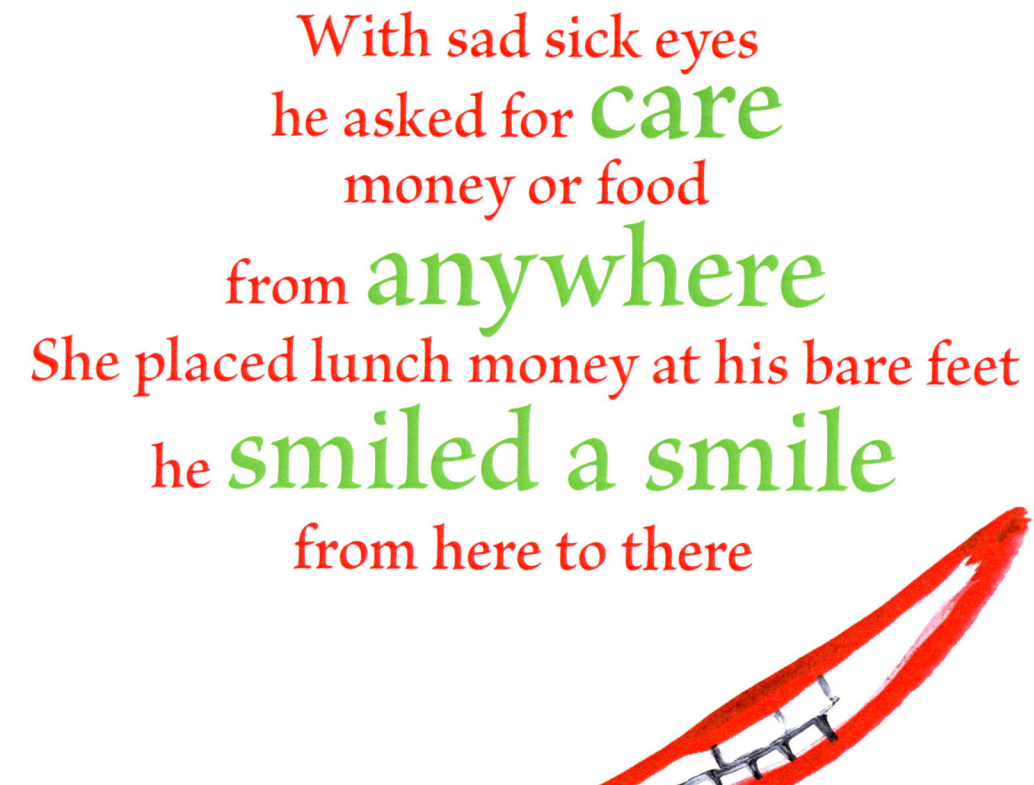

Healed by the wind

sky, clouds, and rain

life is both joy

amidst the pain

All is not lost

For love regains

She lived in a land
surrounded
by seas where wild waves
kissed the morning
and bless you and me with the
love of forgiveness
and all life made free

Her name is our **own**

she is **you**

she is **me**

Her name

is like **ours**

We are God's **Epiphany**

World
without
End.
Amen.

Skya Abbate is a sociologist, Doctor of Oriental Medicine, and graduate of the Master of Pastoral Studies Program at Loyola University, New Orleans. She is the author of five medical textbooks, and is published in her major area of Christian Spirituality and Religion and Ecology with *The Catholic Imagination, Practical Theology for the Liturgical Year,* and *Incarnation, Daily Poems for Advent.* She is also the author of six children's books: *Creation: A Fish Story, Visitation: A Bird Story, Communion: A Desert Story, Vesper: A Horse Story,* and *Ascension: A Swallow Story.*

Skya raises fancy goldfish for fun, loves birds, and lives in the desert and dreams of the ocean.